AN ARCTIC COMMUNITY

Bobbie Kalman
&
William Belsey

The Arctic World Series

Crabtree Publishing Company

The Arctic World Series
Created by Bobbie Kalman

Editor-in-Chief:
Bobbie Kalman

Writing team:
William Belsey
Bobbie Kalman
Janine Schaub
Christine Arthurs

Photographs:
William Belsey
(see page 56 for other
photo credits)

Managing Editor:
Janine Schaub

Editors:
Christine Arthurs
Shaun Oakey
Tilly Crawley

Design:
Heather Delfino

Computer layout:
Christine Arthurs

Map: Chrismar Mapping Service

Printer:
Bryant Press

Cataloguing in Publication Data

Kalman, Bobbie, 1947-
An Arctic community

(The Arctic world series)
Includes index.
ISBN 0-86505-147-X (bound) ISBN 0-86505-157-7 (pbk.)
1. Rankin Inlet (N.W.T.) - Social life and customs - Juvenile literature. 2. Anthropo-geography - Arctic regions - Juvenile literature. I. Belsey, William, 1958- . II. Title. III. Series: Kalman, Bobbie, 1947- . The Arctic world series.

FC4199.R36K34 1988 J971.9'2
F1110.5.R36K34 1988'

For the people of Rankin Inlet

Special thanks to: Ken Faris for his groundwork in the series; the residents of Rankin Inlet who appear in the photographs; the students of Maani Ulujuk School for their delightful contributions; the Pokiak family; Robin Brass for his desktop publishing advice and linotronic output; Arnie Krause for his continuing support.

350 Fifth Avenue
Suite 3308
New York
N.Y. 10118

120 Carlton Street
Suite 309
Toronto, Ontario
Canada M5A 4K2

Contents

We live in an arctic community

If you do not live in the Arctic, you might wonder how anyone could survive in such a cold place. Living in the far north can certainly be difficult, but most residents wouldn't live anywhere else. Read what these school children say about their home, Rankin Inlet, and find out more about the fascinating Arctic.

Lots to do

"In winter there are about four meters of snow and four and a half hours of daylight. There are lots of things to do like hockey, sliding, skating, curling, and playing in the snow. In summer there are twenty hours of sunlight. I go for picnics with my family or friends. There are lots of friendly people."
Tara Lee Campbell

I don't know why!

"Once my dad and I went hunting for ptarmigan. We caught sixteen of them, and the next time we went we caught nothing. I don't know why!"
Benjy Kusugak

Fishing with my mom

"Me and my mom go fishing. Once my mom got a fish and it was a really big fish. She pulled it up and I was happy. We started going home and went to the skidoo and I saw a caribou. My mom shot the caribou and we put it on the *qamutiik*." *Isidore Komaksiutiksak*

Think again!

"The houses don't have basements and are built on short pillars because there is ice under the ground. So, if you think we all live in igloos and caribou skin tents, you are wrong.

"One of the farthest-flying birds called the arctic tern spends its summers in the north. The polar bear is another wonder. If you think the north is a terrible place to live—think again!"
Shirley Rose Fortowsky

My father, the great hunter

"I think of my father as a great hunter. Sometimes he takes the family hunting but only on weekends because he has to work and we have to be in school.

"My father can carve. He made really nice rings for my mom. He also makes *ulus* for my mom and grandma. I wish to carve and make ulus when I grow up. My father also cooks when my mom is away and even when she is at home."
Jamie Makpah

Sliding on hills

"We have no trees, and we have a little animal that runs very fast. It is a ground squirrel and we call it *siksik*. We have a white owl. It is hard to see but if you are careful, you can spot it.

"When it starts to snow, it does not stop for a long time. We have big hills and, if it is not too cold, we get our sleds and go sliding on the hills."
Josh Adams

Where is the Arctic?

The Arctic is a very cold place located in the most northern part of the world. If you look at the globe, you can see just how big it is. It is part of two continents, North America and Eurasia, and seven countries share its vast wilderness. They are Canada, the United States, Greenland, Norway, Sweden, Finland, and the U.S.S.R.

The Arctic Circle

The Arctic begins at the North Pole, but where does it end? Some people say that the Arctic Circle is its correct southern boundary, but just as many think that the tree line is the natural boundary of the Arctic.

The tree line

To reach the Arctic from the south, you travel north through great evergreen forests. The farther north you go, the smaller and more scattered the trees become. The tree line is the area where the trees start growing farther apart and look thin and scrawny. Then there are no trees at all. Where the trees end, the tundra begins.

Small plants, lichens, and mosses cling to life on the rocky tundra.

The frozen tundra

Tundra comes from the Finnish word *tunturi*, meaning "barren land." Trees do not grow on the tundra for several reasons. The climate is too cold. The ground is frozen, so roots cannot grow down deep enough. There is also very little water and not enough light in winter. Trees cannot grow under any of these harsh conditions! That is why people call the tree line the boundary of the Arctic. The farther north you travel, the colder and darker it gets in winter. The land and sea are covered in snow and ice that never melt, and winter darkness stretches for months without a glimmer of light!

The farther north you go, the smaller and more scattered the trees become.

The midnight sun.

A winter blizzard in Rankin Inlet.

In summer the land is covered with ponds. Is the water warm enough for swimming? Brr!

The Arctic is...

...winter darkness

For about eight months of the year the Arctic is dark for much of the day and night. The darkest day of the year is on or around December 21, the winter solstice. At this time the people who live north of the Arctic Circle do not see the sun rise at all. That is why many people feel that the Arctic Circle is the true arctic boundary. In areas south of the Arctic Circle, the sun rises for a few hours around noon each day, and the rest of the day is dark. Children come to school in the dark and go home in the dark. How might such long hours without sunlight make people feel?

...the land of the midnight sun

In summer, on the other hand, the sky is never totally dark. Above the Arctic Circle on or around June 21, the summer solstice, the sun does not set. It does not stay high in the sky but hugs the horizon. Even in the areas just south of the Arctic Circle, where the sun may no longer be visible, its rays still light up the sky.

...freezing weather

In the winter the average temperature is -30°C. Even in summer the temperature drops as low as -5°C. Very little rain or snow falls, but roaring winds can whip up a blizzard very suddenly. People can easily lose their way just walking a few meters between buildings! If a storm begins to blow during a school day, parents are asked to come for their children. Winter darkness combined

with blowing snow makes it impossible to find one's way. Each year several people lose their sense of direction in blizzards and die from the cold.

...permafrost

The ground in the Arctic is frozen solid, as deep as several kilometers in some places. Most of this ground remains frozen all year. Only a thin layer of soil at the top melts in the spring.

...spectacular scenery

Not all of the Arctic is flat. In some of the coastal areas, where the land meets the sea, there are mountains, fiords, and spectacular ice formations. The Arctic is one of the few wilderness areas left in the world.

...a challenging place to live

Living in the Arctic can be difficult at times. Small things that people in more southern places are used to doing, such as making a salad for lunch, playing outside at recess during winter, or driving from one town to another, can be difficult, expensive, or even impossible to do in the Arctic. Yet most arctic residents love their home!

Cape Dorset

Most northern communities are made up of Inuit and non-Inuit residents.

Arctic peoples

Many groups of people live in the Arctic. Some have moved there from more southern places and some have lived there for thousands of years. The people who have been there for a very long time are called aboriginal people. Another word for aboriginal is native. Some of the native peoples of the Eurasian Arctic are called Chukchi, Nenets, Yakut, Saami, and Khanti.

The Dene

The native peoples of the North American Arctic are the Inuit, Aleut, and many different native Indian tribes.

The largest group of native Indians, called the Dene, is made up of seven tribes that all speak similar Athapaskan languages. The word "dene" means "the people" in each of their languages. Most Dene live in the interior towns and settlements of the Arctic, although some live in coastal areas as well.

The Inuit

The largest group of North American arctic peoples is the Inuit. The Inuit live in the coastal regions of the Arctic. They hunt seals, caribou, and whales. They also trap and fish for their food. The Inuit used to be known as Eskimos, which means "eaters of raw flesh." It is not the name preferred or used by these people. They are now known as Inuit which, like dene, means "the people." However, amongst themselves, they have different names depending on which of the six dialects of Inuktitut they speak. The Inuit of Alaska call themselves Yupik and Inupiat, and those of the western Canadian Arctic are known as Inuvialuit. The native people of the eastern Canadian Arctic and Greenland use the name Inuit. The Inuit of Greenland also call themselves Kalaallit.

Sharing concerns

Although the Inuit live in many different communities throughout the Arctic, they lead similar lives and share many of the same concerns. For this reason, the Inuit Circumpolar Conference was set up so these people could discuss problems concerning their laws, language, culture, and wildlife, and share their views with the rest of the world.

An arctic community

An Arctic Community looks at some of the similarities that Inuit communities share, such as climate, environment, culture, transportation, and services. It also takes a closer view of how the people in one community, Rankin Inlet, live. The children who wrote the pieces on the opening and closing pages of this book are from the Maani Ulujuk Elementary School in Rankin Inlet, and many of the pictures throughout the book are also of this community. So, in many ways, Rankin Inlet represents many Inuit communities.

The people in all arctic communities must dress warmly in winter.

Map of the North American Arctic

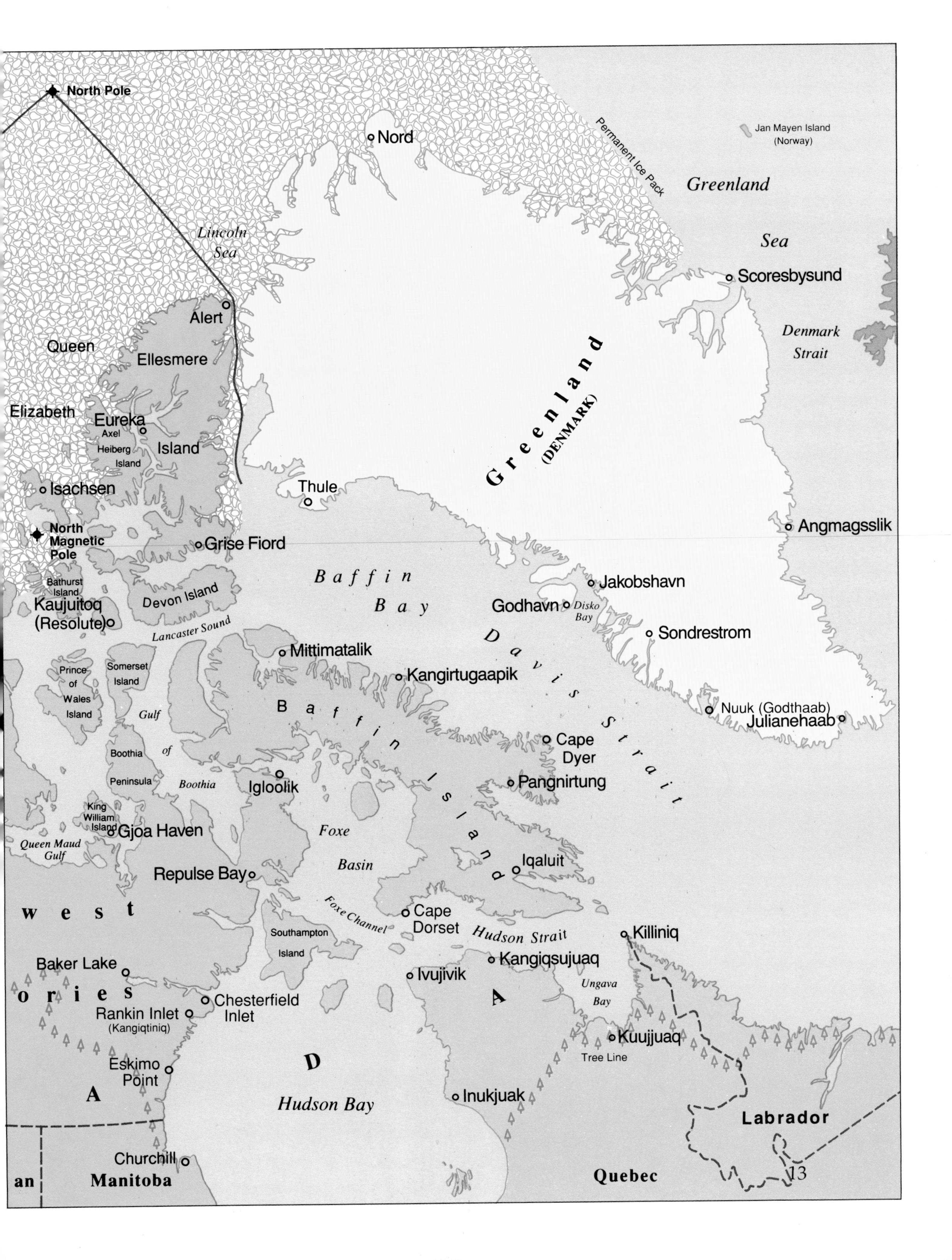
North Pole
Nord
Permanent Ice Pack
Jan Mayen Island
(Norway)
Greenland
Sea
Lincoln
Sea
Scoresbysund
Alert
Queen
Ellesmere
Denmark
Strait
Greenland
(DENMARK)
Elizabeth
Eureka
Axel
Heiberg
Island
Island
Isachsen
Thule
Angmagsslik
North
Magnetic
Pole
Grise Fiord
Baffin
Bay
Jakobshavn
Bathurst
Island
Devon Island
Kaujuitoq
(Resolute)
Godhavn
Disko
Bay
Lancaster Sound
Sondrestrom
Mittimatalik
Davis Strait
Prince
of
Wales
Island
Somerset
Island
Kangirtugaapik
Gulf
of
Boothia
Baffin Island
Nuuk (Godthaab)
Julianehaab
Cape
Dyer
Boothia
Peninsula
Pangnirtung
Igloolik
King
William
Island
Gjoa Haven
Foxe
Basin
Queen Maud
Gulf
Iqaluit
Repulse Bay
Foxe Channel
Cape
Dorset
Hudson Strait
Killiniq
west
Southampton
Island
Kangiqsujuaq
Baker Lake
Ivujivik
ories
Ungava
Bay
Chesterfield
Inlet
Rankin Inlet
(Kangiqtiniq)
Kuujjuaq
Tree Line
D
A
Eskimo
Point
A
Inukjuak
Hudson Bay
Labrador
Churchill
an
Manitoba
Quebec

Clothing

Bundling up against the cold is a task northerners face every day for ten months of the year. When the temperature drops to -40°C, the biting cold finds its way into even the smallest openings in clothing. Long parkas that reach right down to the knees are the most practical coats for this type of weather. Winter jackets and pants made of synthetic materials are worn in and around town, but traditional clothing is still preferred "out on the land" where it is the coldest of all.

The Inuit perfected the skill of staying warm. Their traditional fur boots, pants, and parkas have stood up to freezing blizzards. Clothes made of caribou hide are both toasty warm and naturally waterproofed. In the past Inuit women were highly skilled in using tiny stitches so the wind and water could not get through the seams. They often decorated their clothes with beaded designs.

Nancy Tagalik's son Qajaarjuaq keeps warm inside the hood of her special parka called an amouti. Her older son Tugak stands bundled up in front.

Making traditional clothing takes patience and skill.

The Pilakapsi twins show off their new Easter outfits.

Some arctic buildings are built in a domed shape just like the igloos of the past.

Modern houses are well insulated and energy efficient.

Homes

The permafrost of the Arctic makes building difficult. Houses cannot be constructed right on the ground because the heat inside the buildings would melt the permafrost underneath. The foundations would sink, and the buildings would collapse. All buildings must be built on stilts about a meter off the ground so that their warmth will not melt the frozen ground. For this same reason, arctic buildings cannot have basements. The word "basement" does not even exist in the Inuit language!

Expensive to build

Building houses in the Arctic is very costly because materials are expensive to buy and transport. Skilled construction workers must be brought into isolated areas and are paid high wages for their work.

Homes must be well insulated to protect the occupants from the bitter cold and to help reduce heating costs. It costs much more to heat a building in the Arctic than it does to heat one in the warmer south. When the temperature drops to -40°C and colder, the water pipes inside can freeze and crack. During such weather, no one likes to be the one to fix these ice-cold pipes!

Houses are built on stilts about a meter off the ground. These stilts are driven three or four meters into the permafrost by a machine called a piledriver.

Some people build a tunnel of snow onto the entrance of their house. This snow porch helps insulate the house by shielding the doorway from wind.

Where is that shovel?

Sometimes houses become totally covered in snow during periods of heavy drifting. People who are snowed in cannot get in or out of their houses without a neighbor's help—and a very large shovel!

Although some houses may be covered in snow, no one lives in houses made of snow anymore! However, igloos built in winter and tents put up in summer provide excellent shelter for people on hunting or camping trips.

Many hunters use igloos during hunting trips.

Igloos

At one time the igloo was the winter home of the native people who lived in the central and eastern parts of the Canadian Arctic. Other arctic peoples lived in tents or sod-walled homes all year round. Igloos were never used by the native peoples of Alaska.

A practical home

The design of the igloo was practical. Its domed shape provided a strong foundation and kept heat inside. A skin was hung over the outer and inner entrances to keep the chill out and the heat in. The tunnel entrance prevented the cold from reaching the main living area. To house a large family, a series of igloos were connected by passageways.

Inside the domed living area a snow ledge, or *illiq*, was built about one meter above the floor. Since heat rises, the illiq helped keep the family members warm by raising them closer to the top of the snow house. An oil-burning lamp, or *qulliq*, was placed at the center of the igloo for cooking, light, and heat. The heat from the lamp and the body heat of the people inside kept the igloo at a comfortable temperature. It was warm enough inside that the family took off their parkas and sat on skins.

Even though the Inuit no longer live in igloos, hunters still build them when they must stay out overnight. Arctic communities hold igloo-building contests to encourage and preserve this important traditional skill.

Mariano and Tulimaaq Aupilardjuk show how the entrance of some igloos is dug down into the snow.

A camping stove lights up the inside of an igloo during the winter darkness.

How to build an igloo

The most important condition for building an igloo is having a good supply of crunchy, hard-packed snow that can be cut into sturdy blocks. The Inuit use *pana*, which are long, sharp knives made of bone or metal, to cut these blocks out of the snow. The site of the igloo is also important. The best location is beside a gently sloping hill against which the wind has blown a lot of snow. The snow should be at least one meter deep. This area is used as the pit, or floor, of the igloo. Great skill is needed to make an igloo because the blocks must be shaved at a special angle so that they can be laid down in a spiral shape. The final block at the very top is called the king block, or *qulluti*. The strength of the whole igloo depends on the secure placement of the king block.

◀ *Some churches have been built in the domed shape to reflect the traditional igloo design.*

The blocks of an igloo must fit together in such a way that they lean towards the inside as the wall is built taller.

Transportation

Transportation by plane is often the only way to reach the more isolated arctic communities.

Traveling in the Arctic is a challenge. Starting a vehicle in extremely cold weather and then driving it through a blizzard can be nearly impossible. Specialized vehicles have been developed for travel in such harsh conditions. Bombardiers move well over ice and snow. Many northerners also use three- or four-wheeled all-terrain vehicles (A.T.V.s) to drive over uneven ground in summer and winter. An Inuit corporation is producing a snowmobile designed just for arctic travel. It will be called a Samak.

Although these modern means of transportation are popular, many Inuit still prefer to use the dogsled in winter. During long hunting trips or in very cold weather, a good team of dogs is often more reliable and less expensive than a snowmobile.

No paved roads

Large boats and planes with pontoons bring supplies to communities that are near water. After freeze-up, planes are outfitted with skis so they can take off and land on the snow-covered lakes and tundra. Using long, motor-powered canoes is the most common way of traveling through ice-free water.

Overland travel from one community to another is rarely done by road and never by rail. The heaving ground, spring flooding, and winter snow-drifting make the construction and maintenance of paved arctic highways impossible. The roads in arctic communities are usually unpaved. In spring these roads can become muddy, and travelers often get stuck. In summer, vehicles stir up clouds of dust, so a thin layer of oil or water is sprayed on top.

A dogsled

An all-terrain vehicle

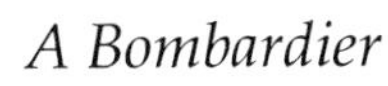

A Bombardier

Water

Every living thing on earth needs water to survive. Plants, animals, and people in the Arctic have learned to adapt to the huge changes in the amount of water that is available. At times there is hardly any water, while at other times water seems to be everywhere.

When people think of a desert region, they do not usually think of the Arctic. With so much snow and ice, it is hard to believe that the Arctic is a dry place. The arctic region is, nevertheless, a true desert because it receives as little as 125 mm of rain or snow each year. When snow does fall, it stays around for a long time. During winter blizzards, much of the snow that is blowing is snow that has already fallen.

Summer waterways

In summer many ponds and waterways cover the tundra. They are not the result of too much rain. They are from melting snow and ice. Meltwater stays on the land for two reasons. The cool summer temperatures cause very little evaporation, and the permafrost prevents water from seeping into the ground. Without the summer meltwater, there would not be enough moisture to keep animals, plants, and insects alive during the growing season.

Water for drinking

All the birds, animals, and people that spend their winters in the Arctic must cope with the lack of fresh water. Animals and birds adjust their diets to

The sea is another source of drinking water. Thawing and refreezing causes the salt in the upper layers of sea ice to sink. Northerners collect and melt these top salt-free layers and use the fresh water for drinking.

conserve water. People have learned to melt freshwater snow and ice for drinking. In many northern communities people store spring meltwater in tanks and then transport it to houses in insulated pipes or by truck during the winter. Meltwater provides a welcome change from chlorinated water.

In early spring, before much melting has taken place, arctic communities usually find their water supply getting low. When this happens, their tap water turns a brownish color because the water level in the town reservoir is down to the mud in the bottom. Sludge gets sucked into the water system until fresh meltwater is pumped into the empty tank.

Once the snow has melted, there is water everywhere. For a few weeks roofs leak, streets flood, and no one goes anywhere without wearing a good pair of rubber boots!

During the break-up of ice in spring, it is often necessary to jump over passages of open water, called leads.

Harry Gibbons is a member of the Rankin Inlet volunteer fire department.

Services

The members of every community share common needs. The people, buildings, energy, and machines that fulfill these needs are called services. Health clinics, police forces, fire departments, and libraries are all examples of services. Some arctic services are the same as those found in other communities, but many are specialized to fit the needs of this unique environment.

A diesel engine supplies energy to generate electric power.

Electricity

Power generating stations provide northern communities with electricity. Electricity is produced by diesel generators. In bad weather, planes and barges cannot deliver fuel to isolated areas. When the town fuel supply runs out, there is a power shortage, so families keep lots of candles and oil lanterns on hand.

The utilidor

Some communities are connected to a utilidor, while others are serviced by trucks. The utilidor, which is a system of pipes, takes away the sewage and provides homes with water. The pipeline runs above the ground or in shallow trenches. It cannot be buried underground because of the permafrost. The pipes must be insulated so that the water and sewage do not freeze. Because of the utilidor's high cost, most communities receive water and send away sewage by truck.

In a medical emergency, patients are transported in a "medivac plane" to a town with a hospital.

A water truck makes a delivery to a house not on the utilidor system.

Water and sewage trucks

Houses that are not on the utilidor system must have water tanks and sewage tanks. When their water supply runs low, a water truck comes to fill it up. And people know that it is time to call the sewage truck when the full tank begins to smell! Sewage is sucked out of the tank by a hose and is taken to a site outside the town limits. Houses without flush toilets depend on a different disposal system. Sewage is collected in strong bags that are picked up by the famous "honeytruck." And you thought that taking out the garbage was a chore!

The "honeytruck" picks up bags filled with human waste.

Snow removal equipment gets almost ten months of heavy use in arctic communities.

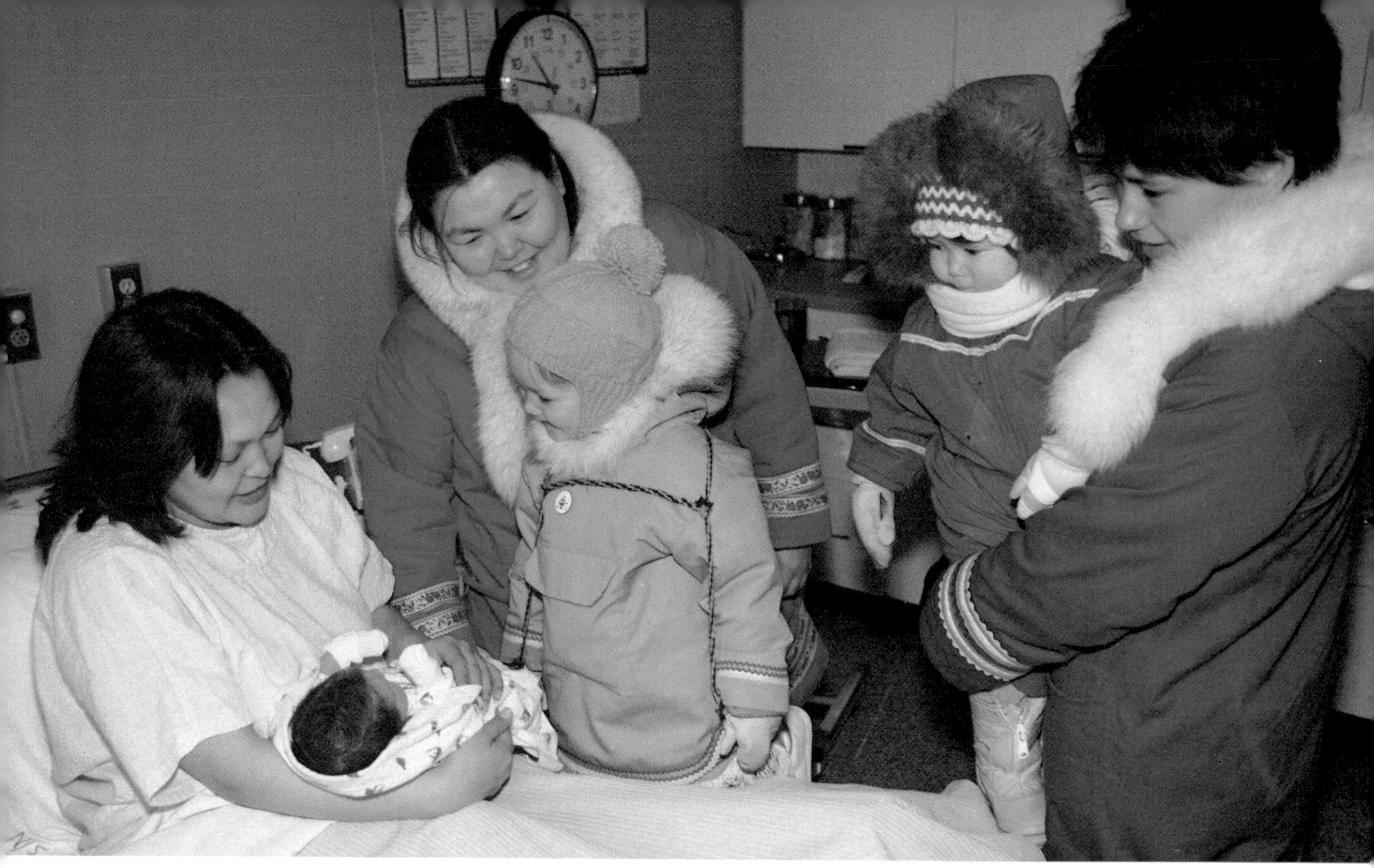

Joan Friesen holds her new baby, Maria, who is only a few hours old. She was born at the nursing station in Rankin Inlet.

An Iqaluit patient's toes are kept warm by a fur sock.

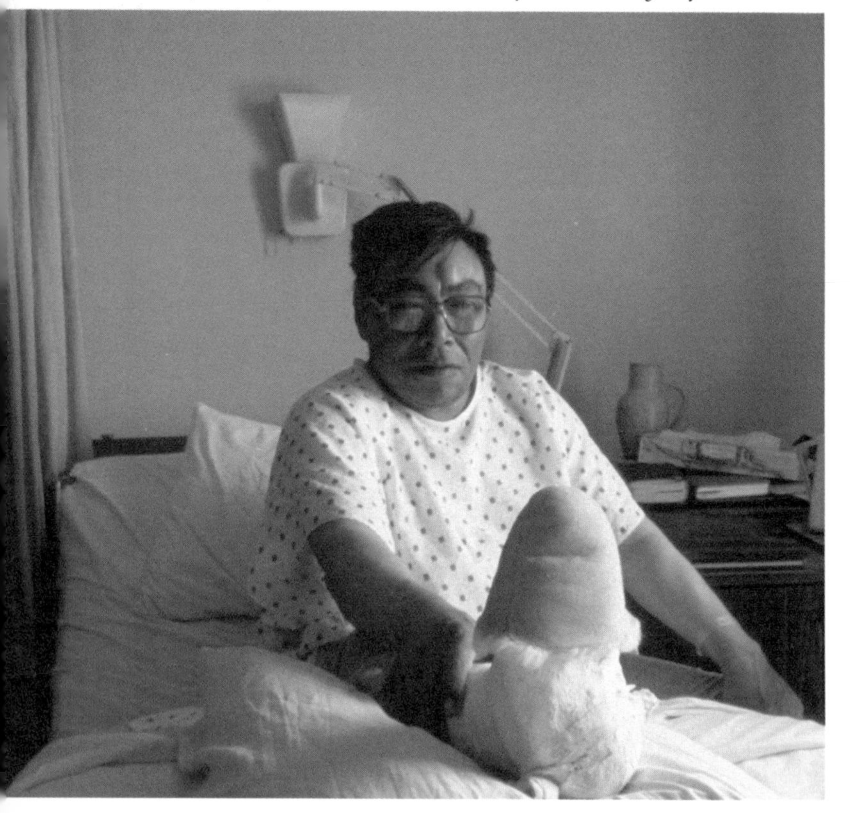

A young patient is cheered up by a ukelele.

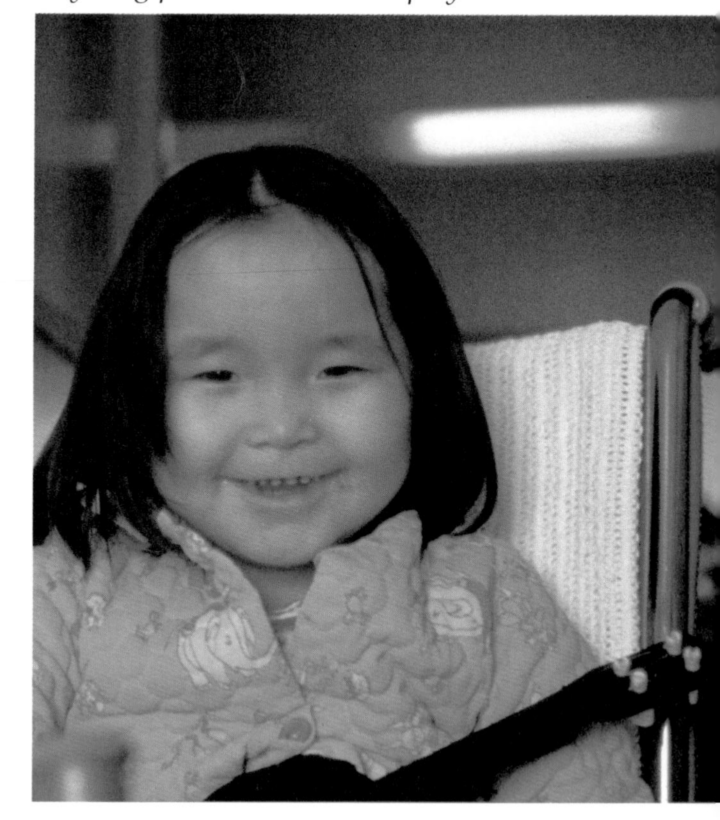

Health care

Health problems in the north are similar to those found in more southern places. People break arms and legs and get colds, flus, tonsillitis, and appendicitis. Nosebleeds are also common because the air is so dry. Eating junk food has caused tooth decay. Tooth decay was unknown to the Inuit when they ate only their traditional, natural foods.

In recent years, there have been more and more cases of lung cancer in the north because many Inuit start smoking at a very young age. Some also chew tobacco, which can cause mouth and gum cancer. Drinking too much alcohol also results in health problems. The Inuit are fighting alcohol abuse by not allowing liquor to be sold in many arctic communities.

Most northern communities cannot afford to build hospitals or to hire full-time medical professionals. Instead, doctors, nurses, therapists, and dentists fly to the Arctic regularly to visit patients. In many settlements there is a nursing station with one nurse on duty day and night. When women have babies, they either give birth at the nursing station or are flown to a town with a hospital.

In a medical emergency, a person is taken to the nearest hospital by a "medivac" plane. For many Inuit, leaving home to receive treatment in an unfamiliar place can be a lonely and frightening experience.

Dental therapist Janet Onalik, her son, and her daughter use puppets to teach daycare children how to care properly for their teeth.

Ranky Pokiak cuts a piece of frozen caribou meat.

Food

If you went grocery shopping in the Arctic, you might be shocked by how much food costs. You could expect to pay two to three times the price you would pay for groceries farther south.

Why is food so expensive? The Arctic has very short summers, frozen ground, and only a few months of total daylight, so most gardening is impossible. Some people have had success growing small quantities of vegetables such as lettuce, radishes, and carrots, but most of these foods come from the south by boat and airplane. The cost of transporting goods to arctic supermarkets makes them very expensive. Although the Inuit buy some groceries, most of their food comes from the land and sea.

Rhoda's bannock recipe

Rhoda Karetak believes that bannock tastes much better while camping out "on the land," but here is her kitchen recipe for you to try. Make sure you have adult help.

Preheat a frying pan at medium high. Mix 500mL flour, 500mL water, a pinch of salt, and 25mL baking powder in a large bowl. Add an egg, some raisins, and a little sugar. Melt a spoonful of lard in the pan. Pour one third of the bannock mixture into pan and cook until small holes appear. Add a bit more lard, flip bannock over, and cook until second side is done. Cut into pieces and serve warm. Recipe makes three bannock loaves.

Try Rhoda's bannock recipe!

Picking and eating fresh bearberries on the tundra is a special treat during the short arctic summer.

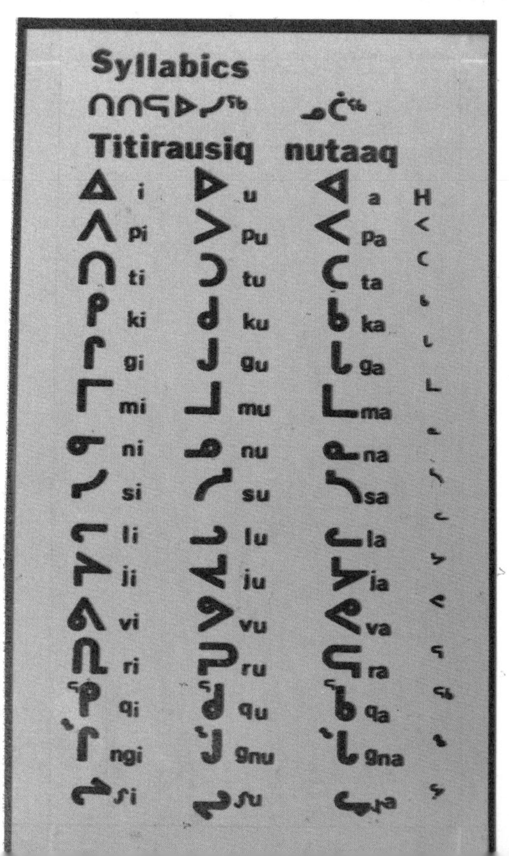

Language

Inuktitut is the common language of the Inuit who live between Greenland and eastern Alaska. Over time this language has developed into six dialects which sound quite different from one another. For example, although both Alaskan Inuit and Greenlanders speak a form of Inuktitut, they would have trouble understanding one another.

Distant relatives

There are similarities between Inuktitut and the Siberian Arctic language, Chukotan. This similarity suggests that North American Inuit are the distant relatives of the people of Asia. It is believed that Asian peoples crossed over the Bering Land Bridge to North America thousands of years ago when the two continents were still connected in the far north by a sandbar.

The written language

For many thousands of years the Inuit passed on their cultural heritage through songs and legends. Nothing was written down in Inuktitut because a written form of the language did not exist. Stories and skills were passed on from generation to generation by word of mouth.

Inuktitut became a written language in the late nineteenth century. Christian missionaries developed a series of symbols called syllabics so that native people could read the Bible in their own language. Syllabics is the written form of Inuktitut that is used by the Inuit of the eastern Arctic. The Inuit of the western Arctic use the regular alphabet to write Inuktitut.

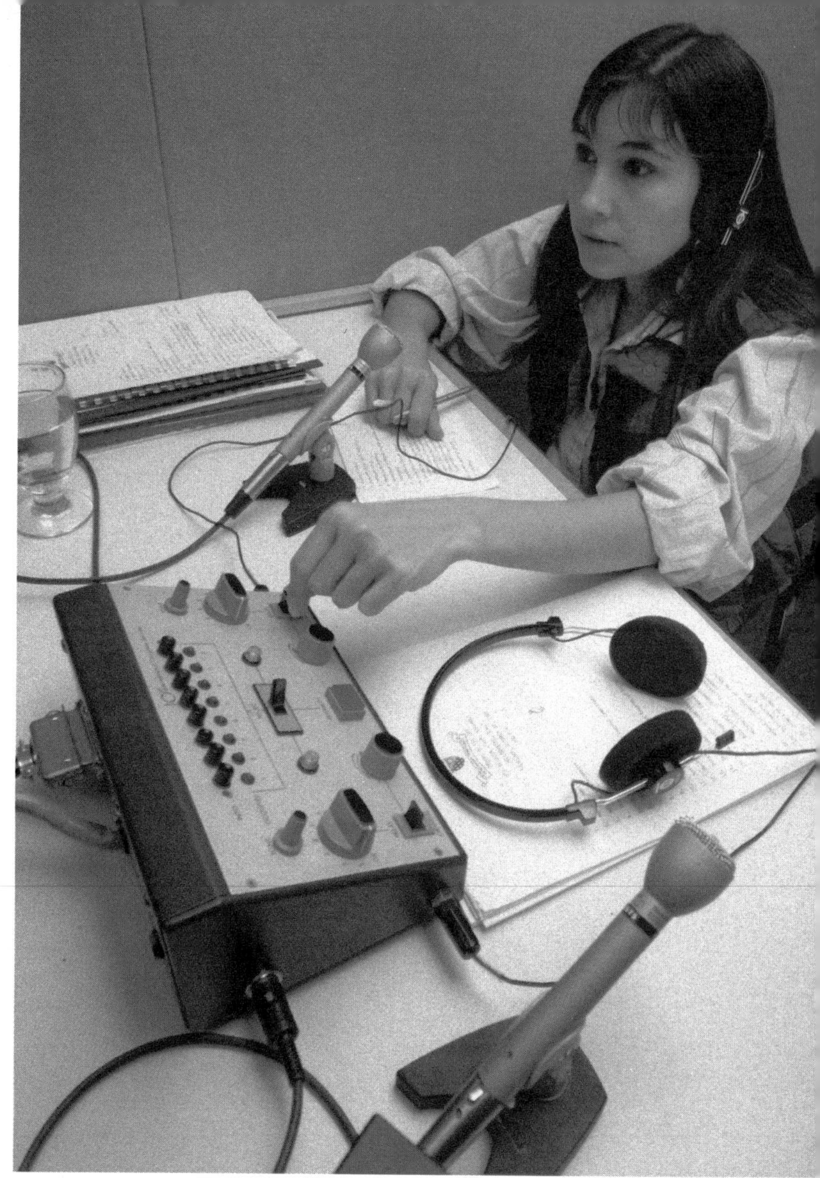

An interpreter translates programs at a local radio station.

Today Inuit children learn to read and write both in Inuktitut and English. The native language is heard on television and radio. Syllabics can be seen everywhere—from street signs to computer screens.

Satellite dishes link arctic communities with the rest of the world. The fence around this one is being used to dry seal pelts.

Communication

Keeping in touch with one another and the rest of the world can be difficult in the north. Communication systems are important because communities are so far away from one another. In many northern towns mail is flown in several times a week. People pick up their letters at the local post office. Satellite dishes also link northern communities to the south by picking up stations from far away. This gives people a much greater variety of radio and television programs from which to choose. Long-distance telephone calls are also made by satellite.

Passing on tradition

Local broadcasting stations provide the community with many native cultural programs. Traditional activities such as hunting, trapping, and sewing are shown on television, as well as storytelling and children's shows. Programs including music, news, and interviews are broadcast in both English and Inuktitut.

Let's talk weather

Radio announcers frequently broadcast the weather because it greatly affects all northern people. Hunters must know exactly what time the sun will rise and set. Weather reports also warn people of blizzards. When there is an emergency, such as a person getting lost, regular programming is stopped until that person is safe once again.

Friendly calls

Phone-in shows are popular in northern communities. People call in when they want to sell a used snowmobile, or when they would like to wish a friend "Happy Birthday." Turning on the radio is like visiting a friend without ever having to go out into the cold.

A television crew films an outdoor concert.

Mail is flown into most arctic communities at least once a week.

This small boy does not seem to like his father's choice of music at this local radio station.

Culture

Artwork, religion, music, legend, and language are all part of culture. Culture is made up of group traditions that are passed on from one generation to another. Inuit culture is thousands of years old.

Inuit art

As traveling hunters the Inuit could only carry belongings that were necessary for their livelihood. These few possessions were both useful and beautiful. The ivory handle of a dog whip, for example, was a delicately carved and decorated tool. In the last hundred years Inuit carving, sculpture, and painting have become popular all over the world.

Singing and dancing

Legends, stories, and songs about life in the past and present make up the Inuit tradition of oral communication. In drum dancing, songs accompanied by the rhythm of the drum and simple dance steps may narrate a traditional legend or tell a story about a recent happening or experience.

New technology

Some Inuit are afraid that contact with southern culture is damaging their traditional values. Others believe that northerners should use new technology to help preserve, record, and develop Inuit cultural heritage.

A native carver files a soapstone in his studio.

Inuit sculptures are displayed in an arctic gift shop.

A performer plays the traditional Inuit drum (atsalauti) in Rankin Inlet.

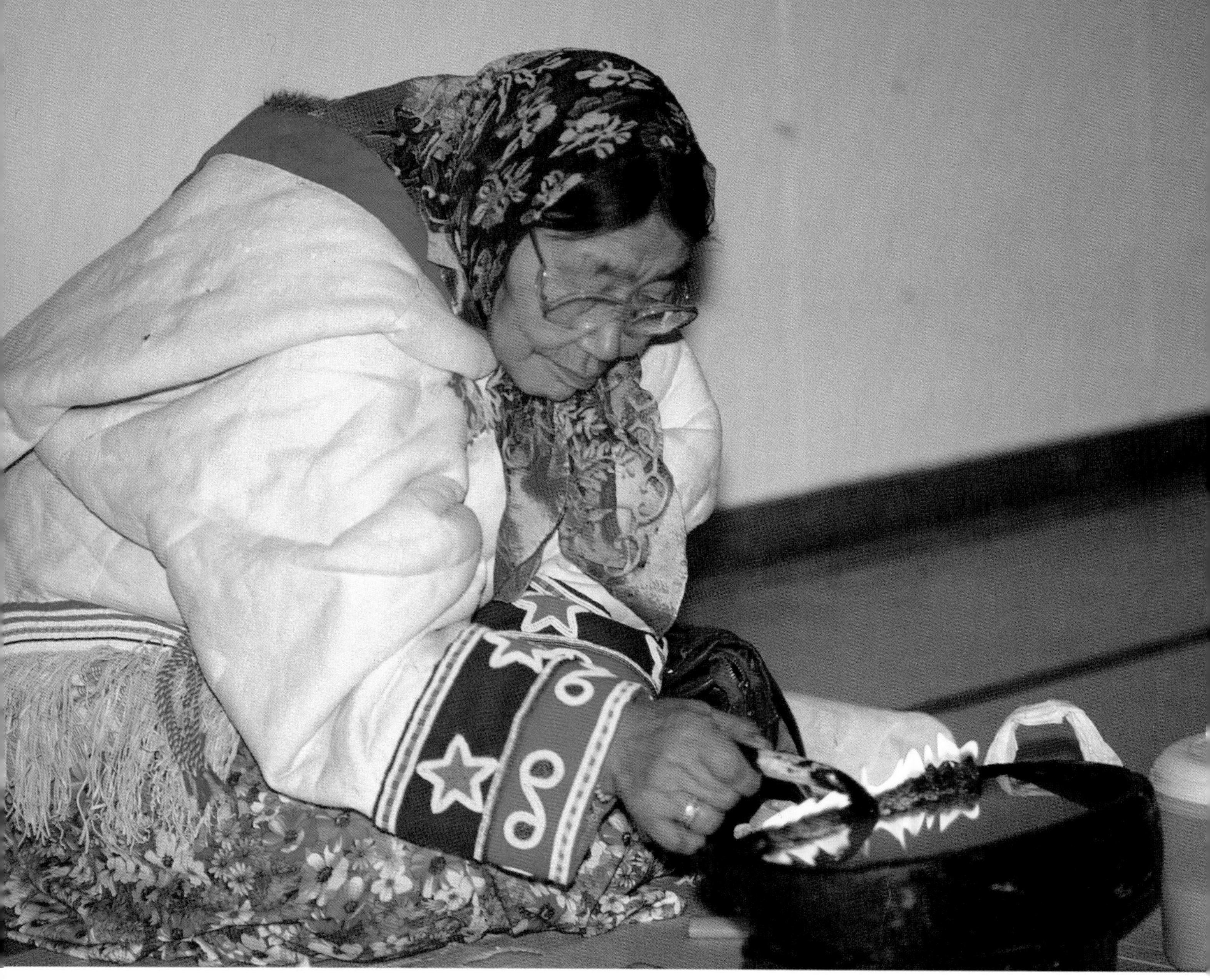

A town elder teaches a class how a traditional stone stove is fueled by whale oil and lit with a cotton-grass wick.

Back to the land

For thousands of years the Inuit have been hunters and trappers. When European explorers came to the Arctic, they introduced the Inuit to new religions and languages and taught them about buying and selling. The newcomers made the Inuit feel that they had to change the way they had lived for generations.

Before too long, Inuit children were speaking English and could not understand the language of their grandparents. Instead of learning their own legends, they were listening to stories about people who lived far away. No wonder the Inuit began to feel cut off from their own way of life!

A new, proud feeling

Today there is a new, proud feeling among the native peoples of the Arctic. Although they now use modern machines and tools, many have started to hunt and trap their food, as the Inuit did in the past. Doing things the "old way" is called "back to the land."

"Back to the land" does not only mean hunting and trapping. It also stands for bringing back the Inuit culture. Being able to drive a dogsled, build an igloo, play Inuit games, and sing and dance in the traditional way are all skills of which the Inuit are proud. The Inuit are also proud of the way in which their people are becoming more involved in government. All northerners look forward to a time when they will be able to take charge of their own cultural affairs.

A craftsman builds a kayak using traditional skills.

Old-style qamutiiks are still used. Today they are often pulled by snowmobiles instead of dog teams.

Pelts are carefully dried and made ready for sale.

A Catholic church with traditional Inuit interior design.

Old and new

The Inuit of today live in a world that is both old and new at the same time. They wear both old-style and store-bought clothing. They eat food from grocery stores as well as food from the land and sea. They work at jobs in town but also hunt and trap for part of the year.

Many changes

Some changes have improved the lives of the Inuit. Hospitals, schools, stores, and airports have all made life less difficult. Permanent homes have allowed people to settle down in one place. New kinds of transportation have given the Inuit the opportunity to follow their traditional way of life on weekends, while keeping their permanent jobs during the week.

Not a nine-to-five world!

Not all changes have been good, however. Living in permanent homes and owning modern appliances are expensive. The Inuit must have jobs in order to afford the modern lifestyle, but there are not enough jobs for everyone. Even when a person has a job, working nine to five while following a traditional lifestyle is not always easy. Sometimes it takes hunters several days to bring home a seal or caribou. Nature's schedule is not the same as that of the working world!

Look carefully! Two children snooze in this sled while their mother finishes the shopping at a local store.

Basketball, soccer, and hockey are common sports in the north, but traditional competitions such as the Ear Pull, High Kick, and the One-arm Reach are still popular. In One-arm Reach all body parts except one hand must be off the ground while the competitor reaches as high as possible to touch a dangling object. The person with the longest reach wins.

Family life

In the past, Inuit children spent all their time with their parents and relatives. As families moved from place to place with the seasons, the children went with them. Parents taught their children the skills they needed to hunt, fish, and trap. Children played an important role. They helped feed the family.

Families were usually large. Even twenty years ago it was common to have between ten and twenty children.

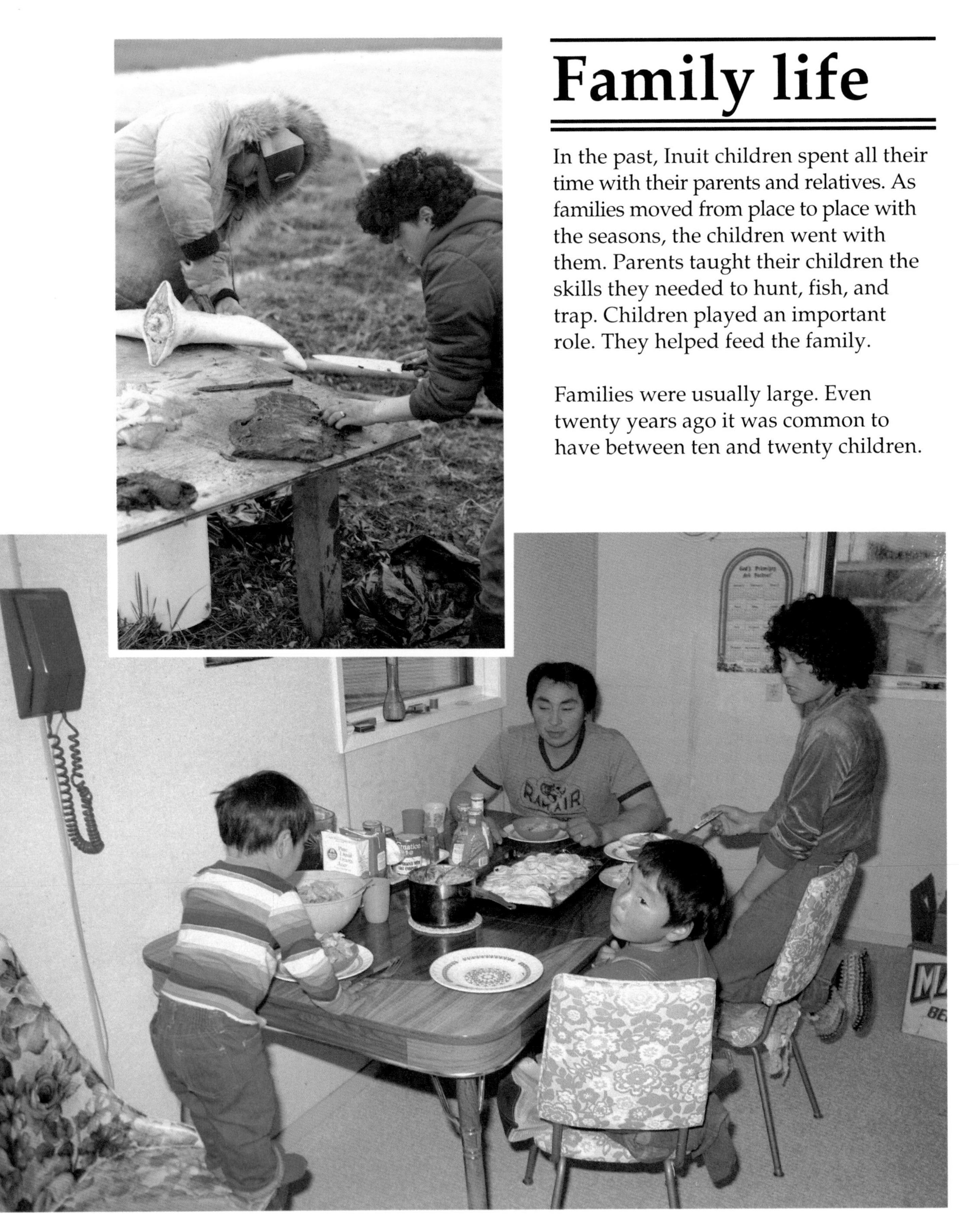

Not only were families large, but uncles, aunts, cousins, and grandparents all lived together.

Although family life has now changed in some ways, families still remain close. Marriages are no longer arranged by the parents of the bride and groom, and couples are having fewer children, but family ties are as strong as ever!

The Pokiak family

Randy and Katie Pokiak and their two children, Lucky and Enoch, are an Inuvialuit family in Tuktoyaktuk, Northwest Territories. Randy came from a family of eighteen children, but he and Katie do not plan to have that many. When he was a teenager, Randy went south to attend high school because his village did not have one. Today he is a successful businessman and often flies south to discuss Inuvialuit affairs with government officials. Even though Randy's job keeps him busy, he puts aside time to hunt and trap. He enjoys providing his family with food while testing his hunting skills out on the land.

Before Katie married Randy, she and her mother worked on the family trapline. Katie learned many hunting skills. She can set traps, skin animals, drive a snowmobile and boat, and shoot a rifle. Katie and Randy combine their skills when they go out on the land to trap and hunt.

Lucky, the older of the two Pokiak children, speaks English, but his father is also teaching him the traditional language, Inuvialuktun. Lucky would

Katie, Lucky, and a friend, Jean Keevik, hang whale meat on poles so it will dry.

rather speak English because that is the language he uses with his friends. Randy hopes that his son will come to see the value of learning Inuvialuktun as he grows up. As well as learning the traditional language, Lucky is being taught the traditional ways of his people. Randy and Katie have been taking him on hunting trips since he was a toddler. Enoch will be ready to go hunting soon, too. After a recent whale hunt, both boys helped prepare the meat and muktuk of the beluga they caught.

Welcome to Rankin Inlet

Rankin Inlet, or Kangiqliniq (can-er-thlee-nik, meaning inlet) is a town on the west coast of Hudson Bay. It is part of the Keewatin Region of the Northwest Territories. Rankin Inlet is below the Arctic Circle, but it is above the tree line, so it is considered an arctic community. Its climate and landscape are certainly Arctic-like!

How to get there

Compared to many other arctic communities, Rankin Inlet is fairly easy to reach. Although there are no roads or railway lines connecting it to southern Canada, there are regular flights from Winnipeg, Yellowknife, and Iqaluit.

Its history

Everyone in Rankin Inlet has moved there from other places such as Eskimo Point, Igloolik, and Chesterfield Inlet. Three quarters of its population is Inuit. Rankin Inlet has only been a permanent settlement for thirty years. Before then, only a few Inuit families lived in the area. For several months of the year these families camped, hunted, and then moved on. Ancient tools and weapons have been found around Rankin Inlet. They show that people have lived there from time to time for more than 3000 years!

In 1928 nickle deposits were discovered near Rankin Inlet. Several years later a mine was built. Most of its employees were Inuit. The town grew as many people from other places came to work in the mine until it was closed down in 1962.

Since the 1970s the population of Rankin Inlet has increased steadily. Today 1500 people live there. Rankin Inlet is now the administrative center of the Keewatin Region. Its government offices deal with the affairs of the whole area.

Its flag

The flag of the Northwest Territories is made up of white and blue panels representing the snow and waterways of the region. The upper part of the shield symbolizes the Northwest passage through the icepack. The wavy line through the middle represents the tree line. The green area of the shield stands for the forested area below the tree line, and the red area stands for the tundra north of it. The important sources of northern wealth, which are minerals and fur, are shown by the golden billets in the green portion and the white fox in the red portion of the flag.

Jobs

Rankin Inlet offers the same types of jobs as those found in many northern communities. The government employs teachers, radio announcers, airport workers, police officers, and mechanics. There is also a growing number of businesses. People work in banks, grocery stores, repair shops, travel bureaus, restaurants, construction companies, and art galleries.

Most of Rankin Inlet's residents live and work permanently in the community, but many are also involved in hunting for part of the year. Unfortunately, Rankin Inlet, like many other northern communtities, has an unemployment problem. Young people find it difficult to get work because they do not have the right training for many of the jobs.

The problem of hunting

In recent years people all over the world have stopped buying products made of fur. Many feel that it is wrong to kill wild animals. As a result, the Inuit can no longer earn enough money from trapping and selling furs to make a living the traditional way. This is a very sad situation for native people. For many Inuit, time spent "on the land" is what life itself is all about!

◀ *Radio announcer Lorne Kusugak prepares English and Inuktitut radio programming for listeners in the eastern Arctic.*

▶ *Peter Ernerk is a member of the Northwest Territories Legislative Association in Yellowknife.*

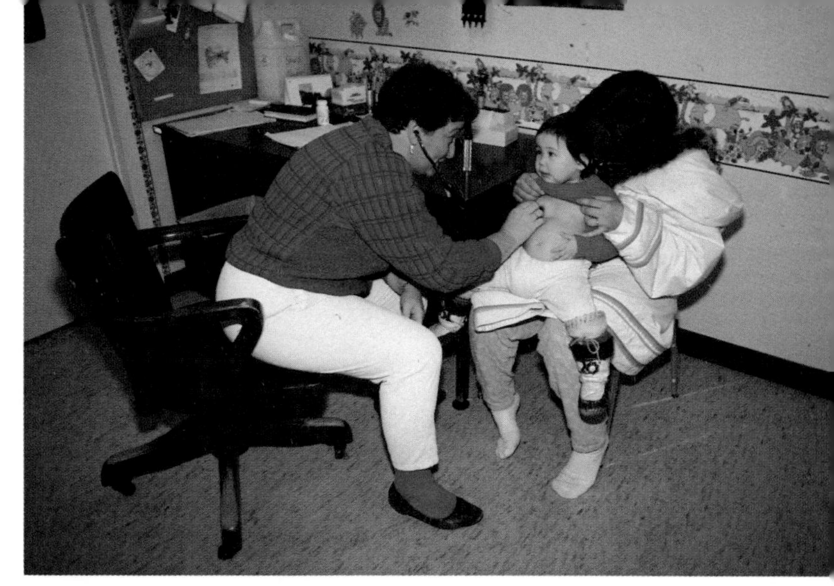

Head nurse Sue Pauhl listens to the heartbeat of baby Bobby Adams at the Rankin Inlet Nursing Station.

Bernadette Tutanuak works as a teller at a local bank.

Two students work on a snowmobile motor in the industrial arts class.

Going to school

The teachers and students of Maani Ulujuk School think their school is fantastic! The school has a large gymnasium with an indoor track. The gym has a stage at one end that is used for school productions. There is a science laboratory, a photographic darkroom, a woodworking shop, home economic facilities, a computer room, an animal-skin preparation room, and even a dental therapist's office. The Maani Ulujuk School houses students from kindergarten to the ninth grade.

High school

The regional high school is also in Rankin Inlet. Grade nine graduates from other communities travel to Rankin Inlet to continue their education. Before this regional school began in 1985, Keewatin students had to live either in Yellowknife or Iqaluit during the school year. Boarding at a regional high school is a common but lonely experience for many Inuit students. After high school, the students who want to go to college or university must attend school in a southern location or take courses by mail.

School's out in May

Today Inuit children spend most of their year in school and learn many traditional skills as part of their school program. The school year has also been adjusted to allow families to go fishing, hunting, and camping during the short summer months. In Rankin Inlet, school starts in August and finishes in late May.

Mariah Alyak's grade three students are learning about money value. They must pick up the amount shown on the card from the coins on the floor.

Alex Komaksiutiksak works on his computer skills at the regional high school.

Students Jeremy Amauyak and Leo Satorsi learn how to make sled runners in the industrial arts class.

In Rankin Inlet there is always someone around who is willing to play in the snow with you.

The people of Rankin Inlet

If you were to visit or move to Rankin Inlet, you would be welcomed by a friendly community. In a short time you would know everyone, and everyone would know you. You would soon discover how willing people are to help one another and to share what they have. Much of your time would be spent attending community events and visiting with neighbors. Here are just a few of the people you might meet in Rankin Inlet!

▶ *Armand Tagoona is an Inuk Anglican minister. His warm smile makes everyone in the whole community feel welcome.*

Michael Kusugak helps make decisions about all of Rankin Inlet's community affairs.

Manitok Bruce (with Coke can) and Jonah Anawak relax on an igloo that was built during the igloo-building competition.

Spring fun

Spring is a special time in Rankin Inlet. The days of darkness are gone, the sun shines brightly, and everyone is happy to be outdoors. People celebrate the warmer weather by holding games and competitions. While some residents are triumphant about winning, others are content to make angels in the snow.

"I got one."

Friendly faces

Rankin Inlet is full of friendly faces. When newcomers arrive in the north, they do not realize that the Inuit use certain facial expressions to communicate. A raised eyebrow means "yes," and a wrinkled nose means "no."

Trick or treat?

When children go trick-or-treating on Hallowe'en, some of their costumes freeze! After calling on homes for treats, the children of Rankin Inlet gather together at the gym of Maani Ulujuk School for the annual "best-costume contest." This year's winner was Brahm Taylor for the most imaginative costume. Can you figure out which hands and legs are his? Earlier that day some children took turns getting their faces soaked as they bobbed for apples. Others baked giant jack-o'lantern cookies. (See page 54.)

Students try out an igloo built during the igloo-building contest over the Christmas holidays.

These students can't wait to sample the Hallowe'en cookies they just baked.

Come visit us!

The children of Rankin Inlet hope that you will become interested enough in the Arctic to come and visit one day. Here are some more selections from their letters. To see who wrote the letters, turn to page 57.

I have forty friends

"In the olden days we used to have igloos. Sometimes we still use them. My dad makes them. We eat caribou meat and fish. I have forty friends and that's it!"
Teddy Ernerk

A very special man

"In the springtime we go out goose hunting. My father lets me and my brother go for a Skidoo ride on the ice. In the summertime we go boating with him to my grandpa's cabin and go caribou hunting and sometimes seal hunting. We also go to the river where we have a tent and go fishing.

"When my father takes caribou or seal home, it is always for the whole family and the relatives. Me and my brother enjoy being with our father. He is a very special man to us."
Jamie Makpah

I love this place!

"There are lots of fun things to do in Rankin Inlet. The first fun thing is sliding. But it wasn't fun when me and my two friends fell off the slide and landed on a rock. The second fun thing is ice fishing. When we went no one got a fish. And the last fun time was when we went on a dog team. A string is tied on some dogs and the sled and you need a whip.

"In the summer people here go fishing, hunting, boating, and baseball playing. I love this place and I don't want it any other way!"
Jackie Price

Would you like to live here?

"Here are some names of animals that live here: siksik, ptarmigan, caribou, fox, and polar bear. Would you like to live here?"
Tara Lee Campbell

Glossary

all-terrain vehicle - A one-person vehicle with three or four wide wheels used to drive over uneven ground throughout the year.
amouti - The fur-lined hood of a special parka in which Inuit women carry their babies.
Arctic Circle - A line of latitude at 66°N, sometimes called the southern boundary of the Arctic.
Bering Land Bridge - A sandbar that connected what are now Russia and Alaska thousands of years ago.
Bombardier - A van that moves along on treads like a snowmobile.
caribou - An arctic mammal with antlers and hoofs that is related to the reindeer.
dialect - A language similar to a common language but with different pronunciation or vocabulary.
Inuvialuit - The Inuit who live on the Mackenzie Delta.
Inuvialuktun - The traditional language of the Inuvialuit people.
kayak - A traditional sealskin canoe-like boat.
lead - A thin, open channel of water in pack ice.
lichen - A non-flowering plant that grows close to the ground on the tundra.
medivac plane - An airplane that is used during the "medical evacuation" of sick people to a city or town with a hospital.
meltwater - Water from melting snow and ice, sometimes saved for drinking.
permafrost - Ground that is frozen all year round.
pontoon - An air-filled cylinder under a plane that helps keep it afloat.
ptarmigan - A chicken-sized arctic bird with feathered feet.
qamutiik - An Inuit sled pulled by a dog team or a snowmobile.
reservoir - A body of water or tank made by people for collecting and storing drinking water.
syllabics - A system that uses symbols to represent letters or sounds.
tradition - A belief, style of art, or way of doing something that is common to a group of people.
tree line - An area where trees grow smaller and farther apart. It is considered by many to be the southern boundary of the Arctic. No trees grow north of the tree line.
ulu - An Inuit crescent-shaped knife used in the cutting up of meat and blubber.

Acknowledgments
Front, back, and title page photos: William Belsey.
Photo credits: William Belsey, pages 4-5, 7(top), 8(center), 14, 15(top), 15(bottom right), 16(center), 17(top), 18(top), 19(top), 20(center), 20(bottom), 21, 24(top), 24(center), 25, 26(top), 27, 29, 30, 31(bottom), 33(top), 33(center), 35, 36, 37(bottom), 38(bottom), 42-56;
Ken Faris, pages 7(bottom), 16(bottom), 23(top), 28(bottom right), 34(bottom), 38(top), 40-41;
Barry Griffiths, pages 20(top), 23(bottom), 37(top), 37(center);
Health and Welfare Canada, pages 6, 8(bottom), 9, 10(top), 10(bottom), 15(bottom left), 16(top), 18(bottom), 22, 24(bottom), 26(bottom left), 26(bottom right), 28(bottom left), 33(bottom), 34(top);
Sherman Hines/Masterfile, page 19(bottom);
SSC-Photocentre-ASC/Photo by: George Hunter, page 8(top);
Jerome Knap, pages 17(bottom), 19(center), 32;
N.W.T. Government/Photo by: Tessa Macintosh, pages 11, 28(top), 31(top), 39.
Girl on cover: Lisa Benoit

456789 BP Printed in Canada 765432109

Index

Front row from left to right: Jackie Price, Jason Pineau, Tara-Lee Campbell, Billy Ross, Janet Foster (photographer), Lisa-Ann Manitok, Tina-Ann Price, Jeffrey Taparti. **Middle row:** Victoria Angoshadluk, Joy Ford, Joanna Nanooklook, Arsene Kapuk, Teddy Ernerk, Josh Adams, Shirley Fortowsky, Ryan Adams. **Top row:** William Belsey (teacher and author), Raymond Mercer, William Robertson, Taina Kubluitok, Stacy Anawak, Glenda Adams, Benjamin Kusugak, Isidore Komaksiutiksak, Tommy Sharp, Jamie Makpah, Gary Sigurdson, Jean Williamson (principal).